BIG BOOK OF
BART SIMPSON

TITAN BOOKS

Dedicated to Burpo:

How you ended up in Kitty Heaven we'll never know.

BIG BOOK OF BART SIMPSON

Copyright ©2000, 2001 & 2002 by
Bongo Entertainment, Inc. All rights reserved.
No part of this book may be used or reproduced in any manner whatsoever
without written permission except in the case of brief quotations
embodied in critical articles and reviews. For information address:
Bongo Comics Group c/o Titan Books
1440 S. Sepulveda Blvd., 3rd Floor, Los Angeles, CA 90025

Published in the UK by Titan Books, a division of Titan Publishing Group,
144 Southwark St., London SE1 0UP, under licence from Bongo Entertainment, Inc.

FIRST EDITION: JULY 2002

ISBN 1-84023-425-3
8 10 9 7

Publisher: MATT GROENING
Creative Director: BILL MORRISON
Managing Editor: TERRY DELEGEANE
Director of Operations: ROBERT ZAUGH
Art Director: NATHAN KANE
Production Manager: CHRISTOPHER UNGAR
Legal Guardian: SUSAN GRODE

Contributing Artists:
IGOR BARANKO, KAREN BATES, JEANNETTE BOSE, JOHN COSTANZA, DAN DECARLO, MIKE DECARLO,
FRANCIS DINGLASAN, JASON HO, NATHAN KANE, CAROLYN KELLY, SCOTT MCRAE, BILL MORRISON,
PHIL ORTIZ, MIKE ROTE, SCOTT SHAW!, CHRIS UNGAR, ART VILLANUEVA, AND MIKE WORLEY

Contributing Writers:
JAMES BATES, GEORGE GLADIR, SCOTT SHAW!, GAIL SIMONE, AND CHRIS YAMBAR

PRINTED IN ITALY

TABLE OF CONTENTS

BART SIMPSON IN:

BIG FAT TROUBLE IN Little SPRINGFIELD

GANG-WAY, PEOPLE! COMIN' THROUGH!

IT'S USELESS TRYING TO OUTRUN THEM, BART! LET'S JUST TAKE OUR WEDGIES LIKE REAL MEN AND GET IT OVER WITH.

STORY	ART	COLORS	LETTERS	EDITOR	LIPOSUCTIONIST
CHRIS YAMBAR	JOHN COSTANZA	ART VILLANUEVA	KAREN BATES	BILL MORRISON	MATT GROENING

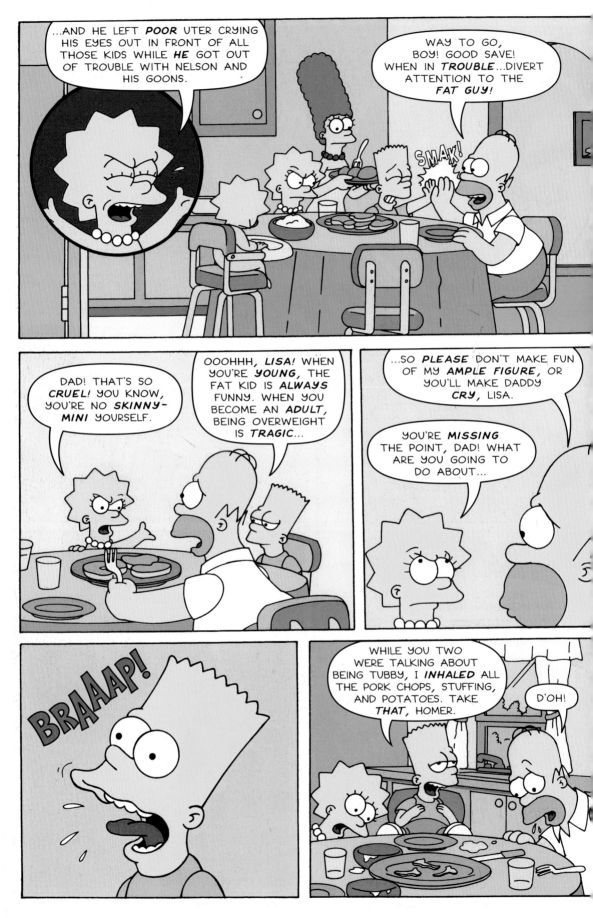

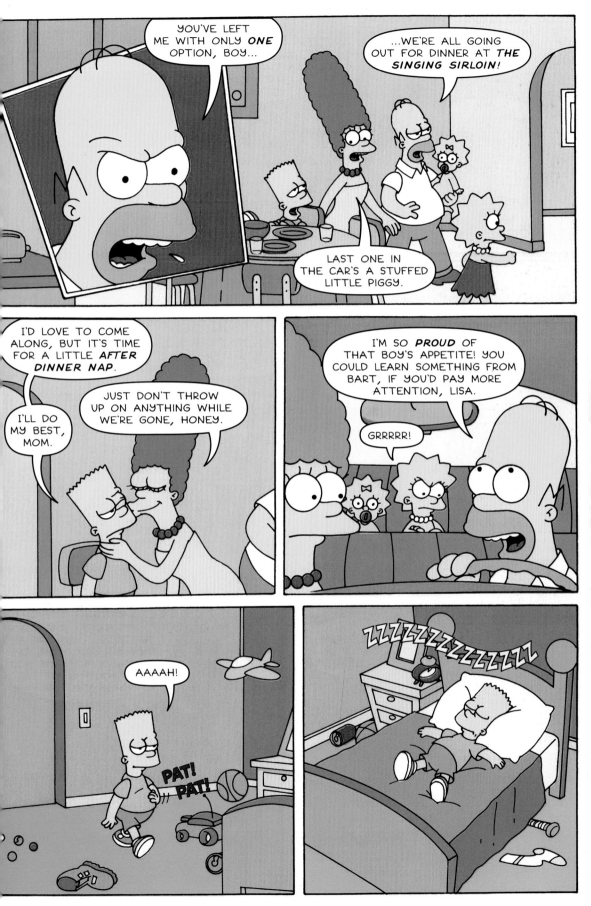

9

14

THE BEER CAN BE REPLACED, BUT THIS TROPHY CAN'T!

HOMER, I WANT YOU TO BUILD A CASE TO DISPLAY AND PROTECT ALL OF LISA'S SOCCER TROPHIES.

D'OH! NOW SEE WHAT YOU'VE DONE?!

WE'RE SO PROUD OF YOU, LISA! EVERYONE'S TALKING ABOUT YOUR GOAL-TENDING TALENTS! WHO KNOWS WHERE IT'LL LEAD TO?

LOUSY, ROTTEN, STINKIN'....

NEWSLEAK
October 4, 2011
LISA SIMPSON
ANOTHER USA WORLD TITLE

IS THERE NO END TO THIS "GIRL POWER"?!

BURPO COMICS

YES WE'RE OPEN

THANK GOODNESS THERE'S STILL BURPO, MY GIRL-HATING, HOAGIE-EATING HERO!

THE END

STORY
GEORGE GLADIR

PENCILS
CAROLINE KELLY

INKS
MIKE ROTE

LETTERS
KAREN BATES

COLORS
BATES/VILLANUEVA

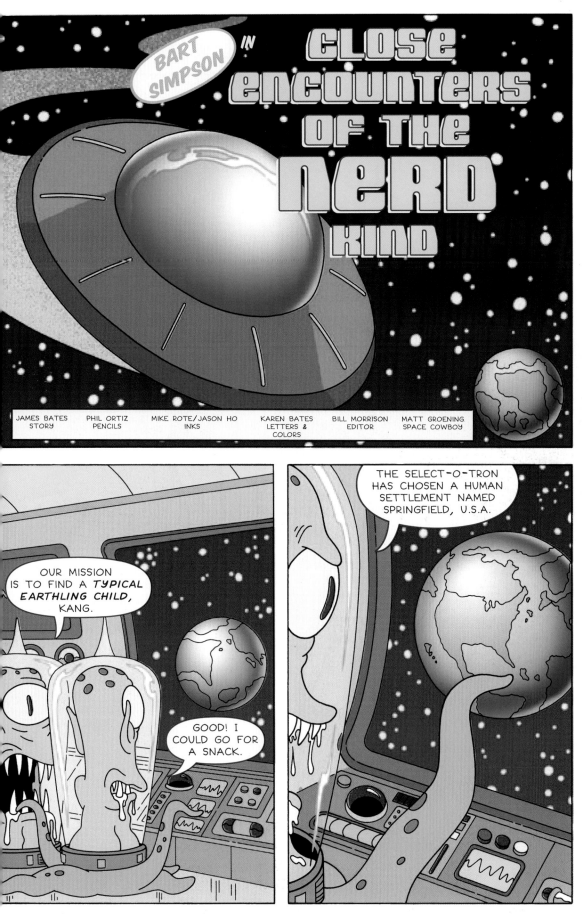

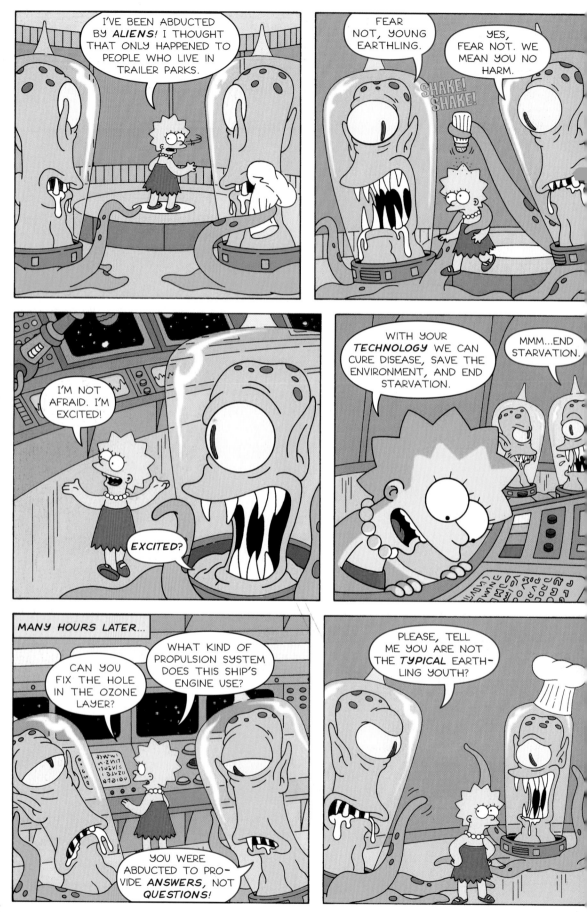

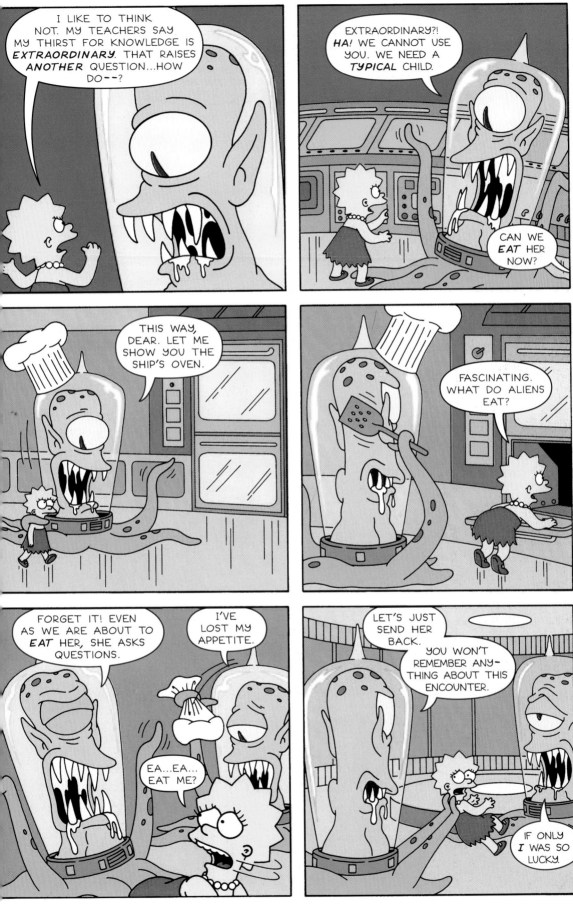

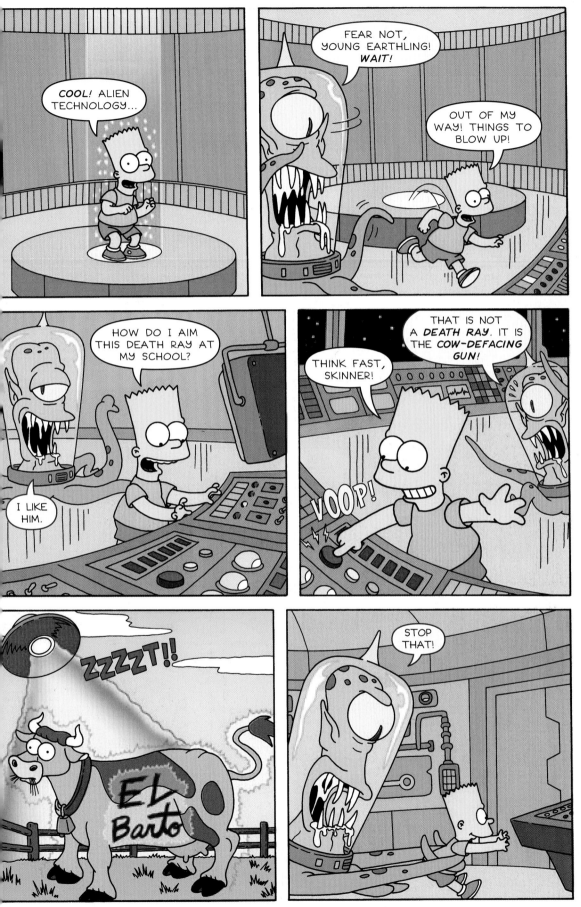

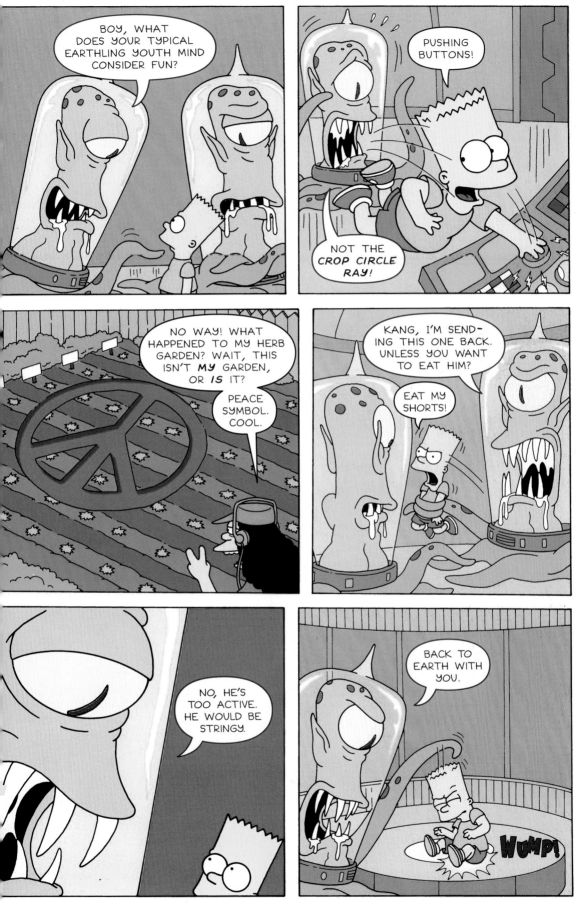

31

BART SIMPSON
IN
BART'S DAY AT THE ZOO

I AM NOT AN *ANIMAL!* I AM A *HUMAN BEING!*

JAMES W. BATES
STORY

IGOR BARANKO
ART

KAREN BATES
COLORS & LETTERS

BILL MORRISON
EDITOR

MATT GROENING
CHAPERONE

AH, A SCHOOL TRIP TO THE ZOO...

...NOTHING LIKE A *FIELD TRIP* TO SHOW-CASE THE MISCHIEVOUS COMIC STYLINGS OF *BART SIMPSON!*

35

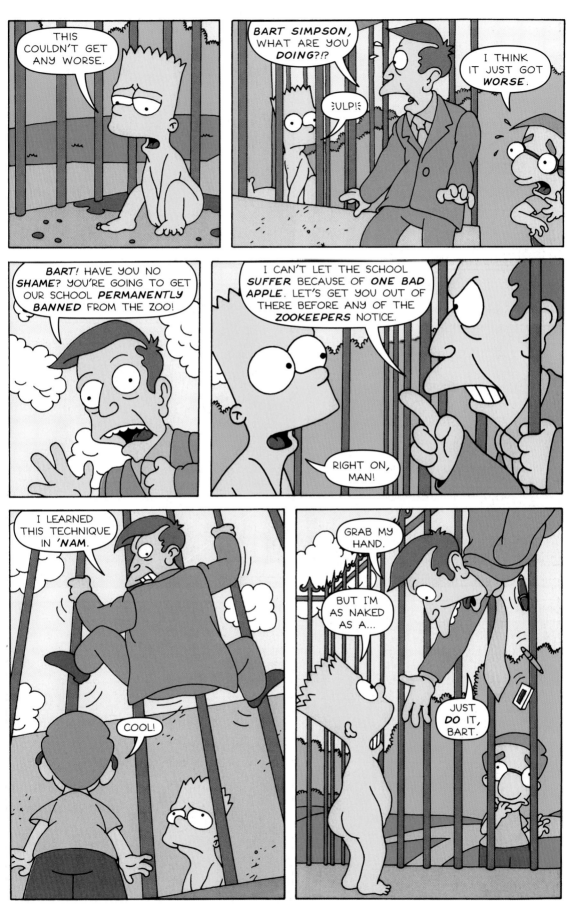

ALRIGHT, DUDE!

DON'T YANK!

WHAT?

OH, MOTHER!

NOT AGAIN!

BART, WHY DO YOU HATE ME SO?

DON'T WORRY. I WATCHED PRINCIPAL SKINNER'S 'NAM CLIMBING TRICK. *I'LL* GET YOU OUT!

THIRTY SECONDS LATER...

IT WAS A *NICE TRY*, MILHOUSE.

WELL, MY LUCKY STARS! FINALLY A *PROUD FRATERNITY OF LOSERS* IN WHICH I CAN JOIN. AND JOIN YOU I WILL, AFTER I CORRECT THIS SIGN TO DENOTE THE PLURAL "*LOSERS*."

EXHIBIT
LOSEr

42

GEORGE GLADIR
SCRIPT

FRANCIS DINGLASAN
PENCILS

MIKE DE CARLO
INKS

ART VILLANUEVA
COLORS

KAREN BATES
LETTERS

BILL MORRISON
EDITOR

MATT GROENING
TALENT SCOUT

45

HOW ABOUT SKATEBOARDING? YOU'RE PRETTY GOOD AT THAT.

PRETTY GOOD? I'M INCREDIBLE! YOU'RE RIGHT, MILHOUSE!

LISTEN TO THE LITTLE WEASEL RAVE!

HE THINKS HE'S A DOCTOR OF SHREDOLOGY!

CAN YOU DO A TRIPLE CORKSCREW?

UH... MAYBE.

MAN, THAT'S FLY!

HOW ABOUT A DOUBLE LOOP-DE-LOOP?

SURE, ≥GULP≤ IF I WANTED TO.

FACE IT, SPIKE-HEAD....

...YOU'RE NO HOT-DOG! YOU'RE A MEDIOCRE SHREDDER AT BEST!

HE'S RIGHT. AND EVEN IF I WAS IN HIS LEAGUE, SO ARE A BAZILLION OTHER KIDS.

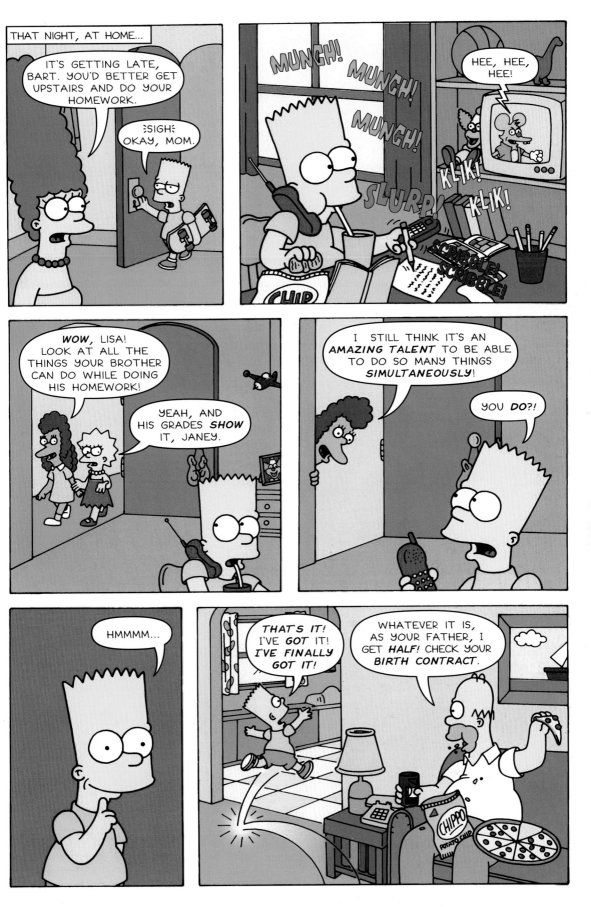

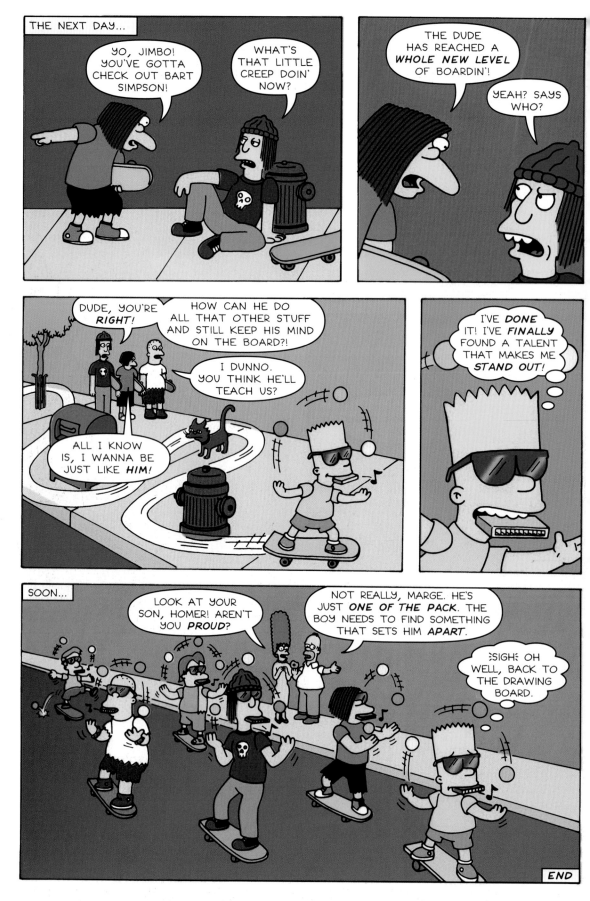

GAIL SIMONE
SCRIPT

DAN DECARLO
LAYOUTS

MIKE ROTE
PENCILS & INKS

ART VILLANUEVA
COLORS

KAREN BATES
LETTERS

BILL MORRISON
EDITOR

MATT GROENING
ONE IN A MILLION

BARTMAN IN "FUTILITY BELT"

HOUSEBOY, I'VE BEEN THINKING. IF I'M GOING TO COMPETE WITH THE SUPER VILLAINS OF THE NEW MILLENNIUM, I'LL NEED MORE THAN JUST THE BART-ROPE AND THIS COOL COSTUME.

L-LIKE WHAT, BARTMAN?

| GEORGE GLADIR STORY | JASON HO INKS | KAREN BATES LETTERS | MATT GROENING COMEDIC CRUSADER |
| JEANETTE BOSE PENCILS | ART VILLANUEVA COLORS | BILL MORRISON EDITOR | |

LIKE THE ARSENAL OF WEAPONS I'VE INVENTED FOR MY NEW UTILITY BELT!

COOL! HOW'S IT WORK?

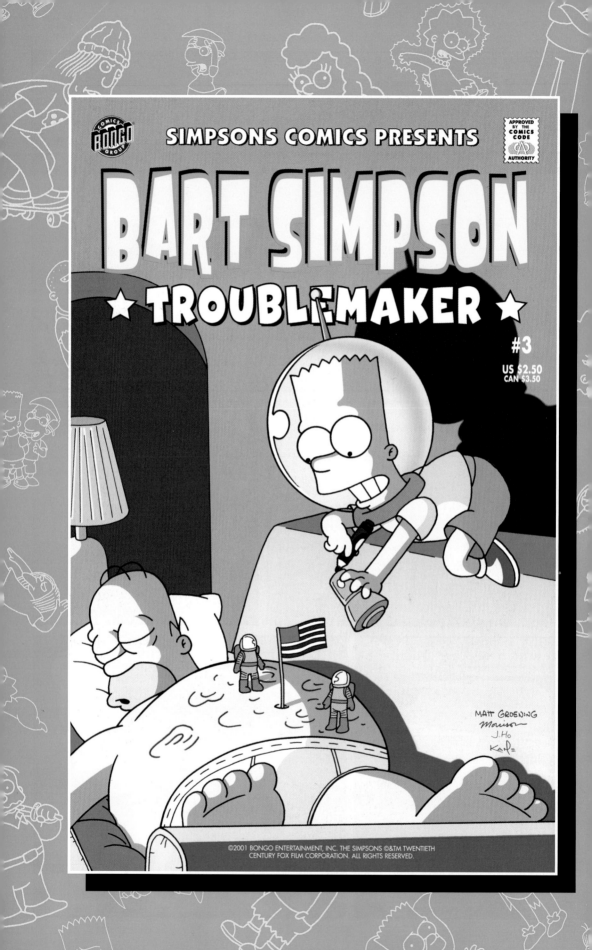

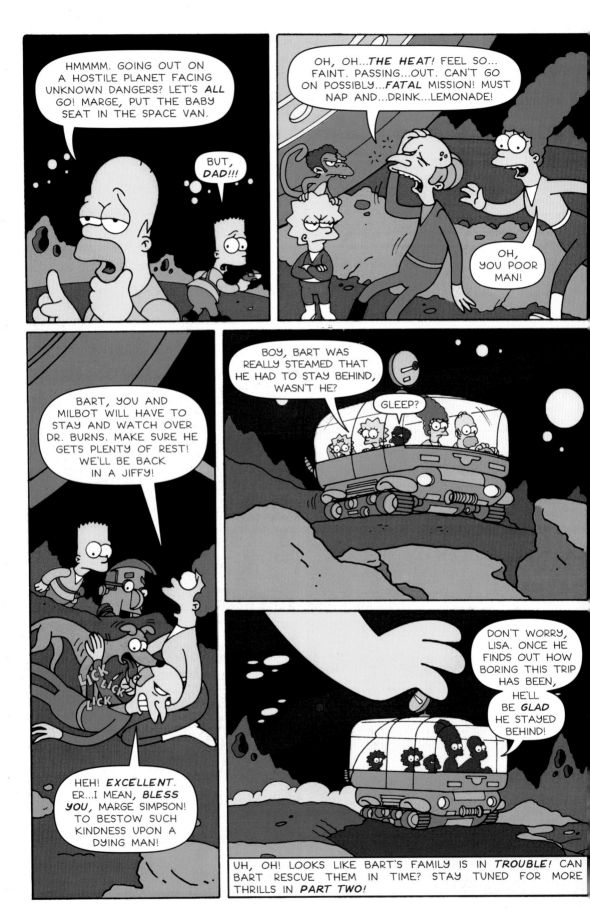

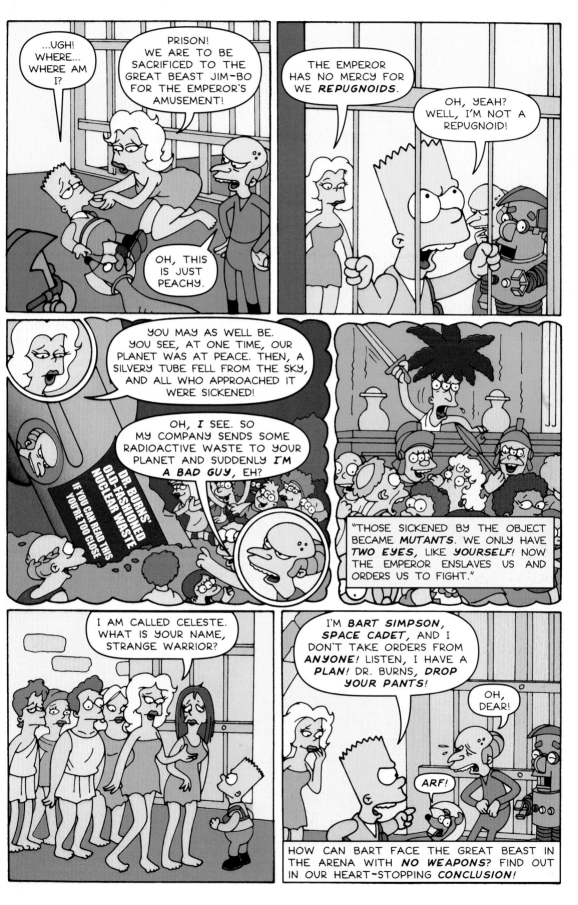

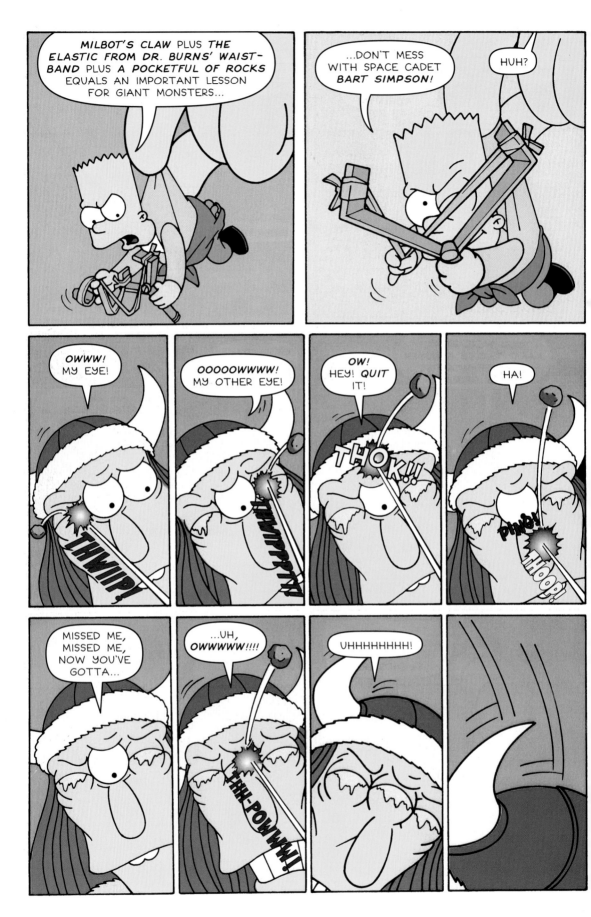

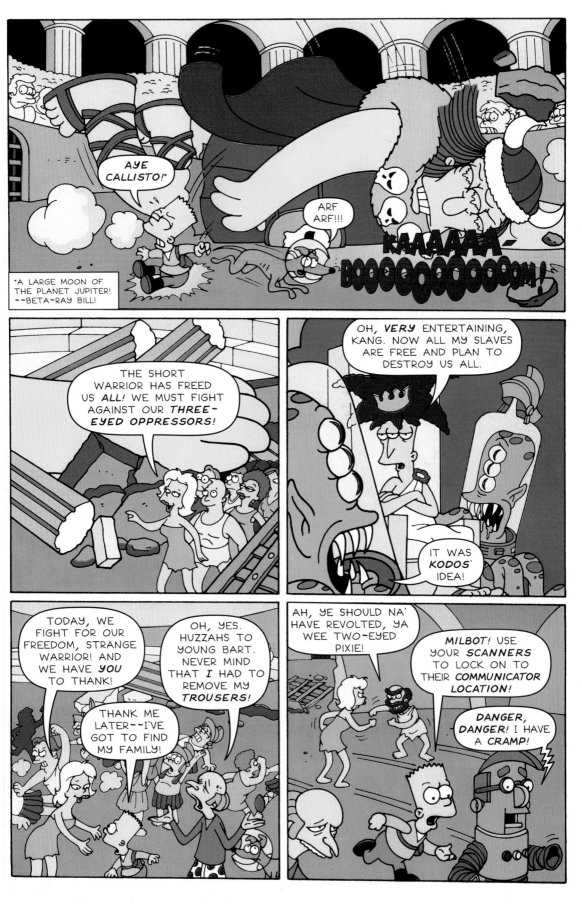

GAIL SIMONE
SCRIPT

DAN DECARLO
LAYOUTS

MIKE ROTE
PENCILS & INKS

KAREN BATES
COLORS & LETTERS

BILL MORRISON
EDITOR

MATT GROENING
NEW KID ON THE BLOCK

BEIRUT, SAIGON, IRAN...THIS REPORTER HAS SEEN *MANY A BLOODY BATTLE* ON TV. BUT NO TV NEWSCAST COULD PREPARE ME FOR THE *CARNAGE* THAT'S TAKING PLACE *HERE* IN OUR OWN FAIR CITY, AS THE TWO REIGNING MALE VOCAL GROUPS IN THE PRECIOUS *10-18 YEAR OLD DEMOGRAPHIC GROUP* FACE OFF FOR WHAT LOOKS LIKE A FIGHT TO THE *DEATH!*

WAIT...*SCRATCH* THAT. IT APPEARS THAT RATHER THAN THE PREVIOUSLY-PROMISED FIGHT TO THE DEATH, THERE WILL BE A "*SING-OFF*" TO DECIDE WHICH BAND GETS LITTLE *LISA SIMPSON* AS THEIR NUMBER ONE FAN!

PFFFT! A "*SING-OFF!*" THAT'S JUST WHAT *NIXON* WANTED AT THE *KENNEDY DEBATES!*

THIS ONE'S FOR *YOU*, LISA!

OH, MAN! COULD THIS *GET* ANY MORE GIRL-FRIENDLY?

YOU ARE...MY LOVE MY LOVE, YOU ARE MY LOVE, YOU ARE MY LOVE, LOVE MY YOU. AM I YOUR LOVE? YOUR LOVE... AM I? LOVE LOVE, YOUR AM I LOVE AM I?

:SIGH!:

GAIL SIMONE
RECIPE

DAN DECARLO
LUSCIOUS LAYOUTS

MIKE ROTE
ALL-PURPOSE ART

KAREN BATES
CREAMY COLORS/LUMPY LETTERS

BILL MORRISON
HEAD CHEF

MATT GROENING
TOP NUT

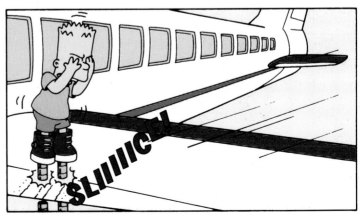

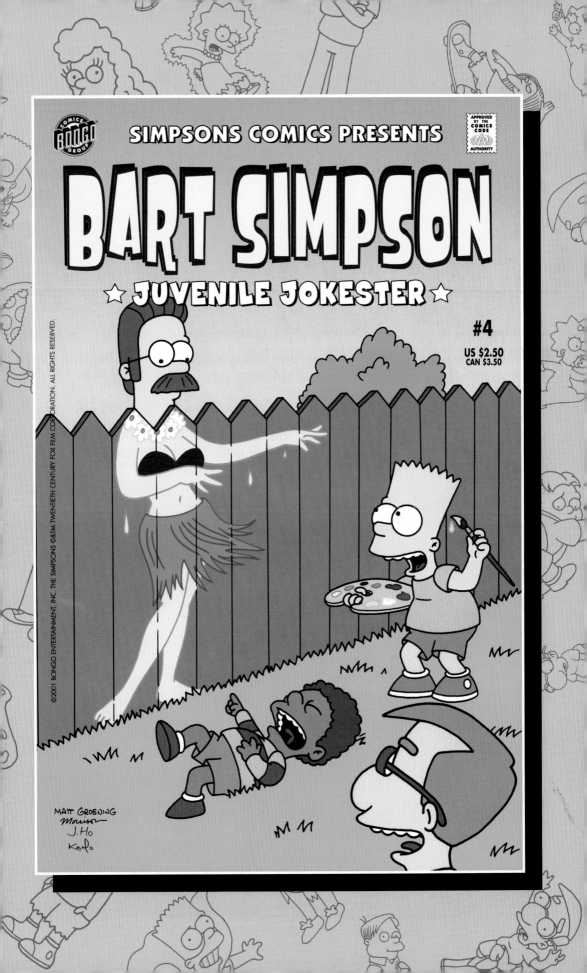

SCRIPT AND LAYOUTS BY *SCOTT "CHUMP CHANGE" SHAW!*
FINISHED ART BY *MIKE "HEY, MY WALLET IS MISSING" WORLEY*
LETTERS BY *KAREN "HIGH ROLLER" BATES*
COLORED BY *ART "LONG GREEN" VILLANUEVA* AND
    KAREN "GREENBACKS" BATES
EDITED BY *BILL "MO' MONEY" MORRISON*
TOLERATED BY *MATT "THE BIG BUCKS STOP HERE" GROENING*

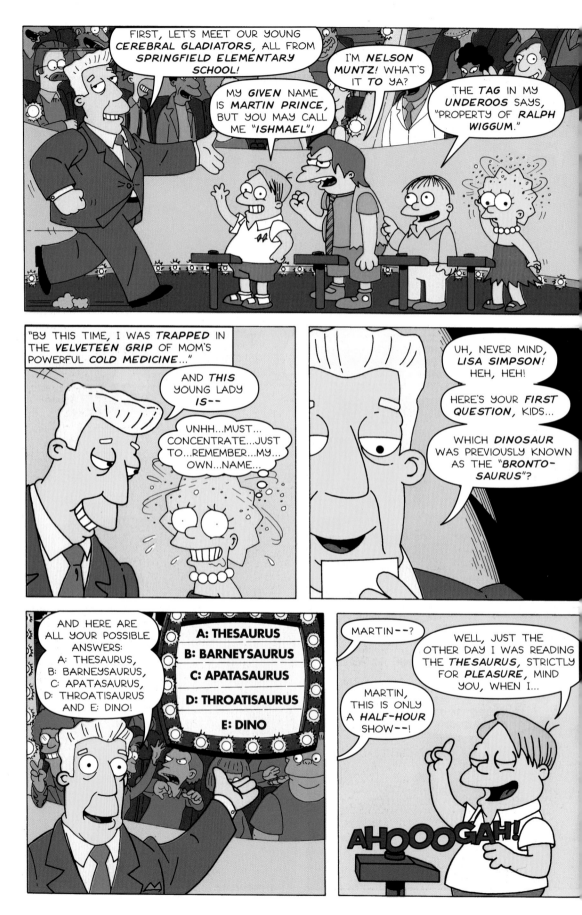

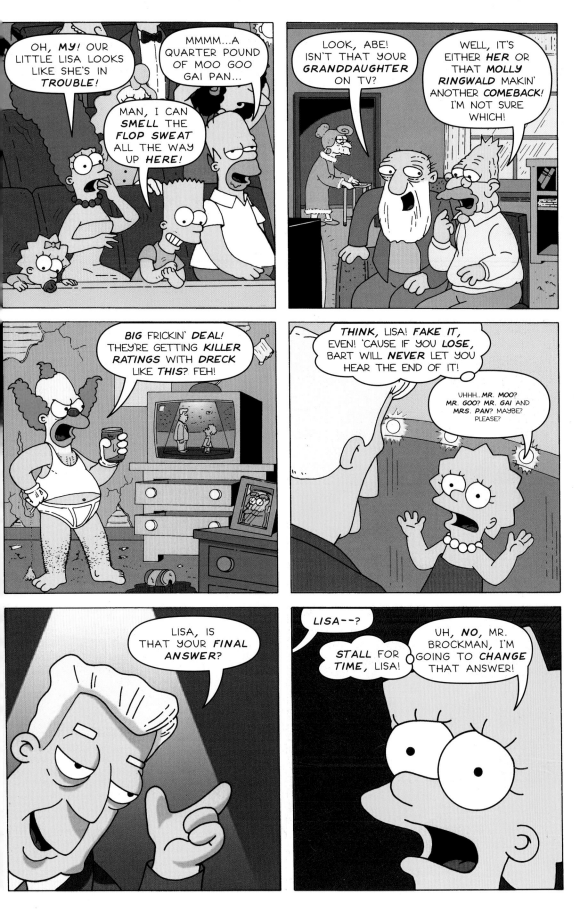

GAIL SIMONE
SODA JERK SCRIPT

DAN DECARLO
LO-CAL LAYOUTS

JASON HO
SIX-PACK PENCILS & FIZZY INKS

CHRIS UNGAR
CARBONATED COLORS

KAREN BATES
LEMON-LIME LETTERS

BILL MORRISON
ALL-NATURAL EDITS

MATT GROENING
BEST BURPS

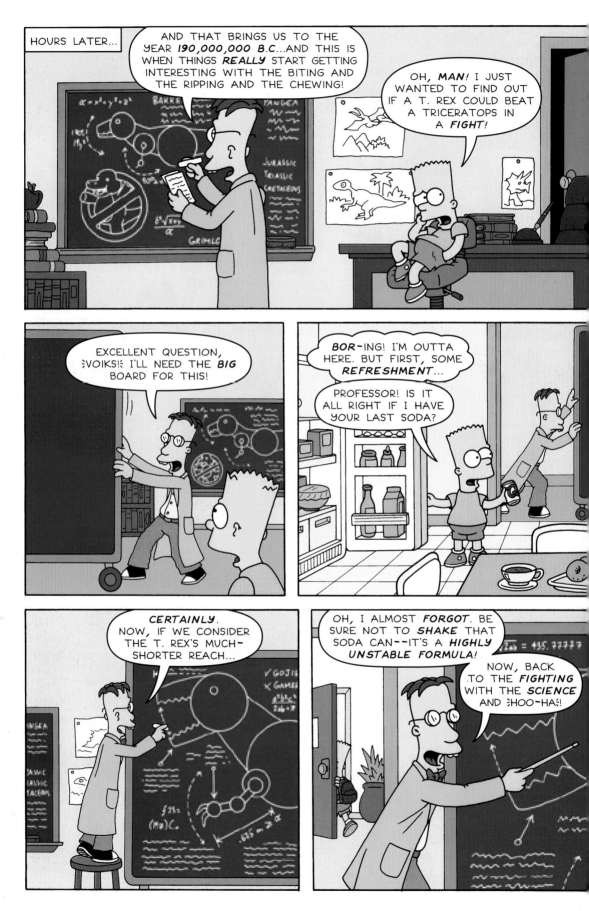

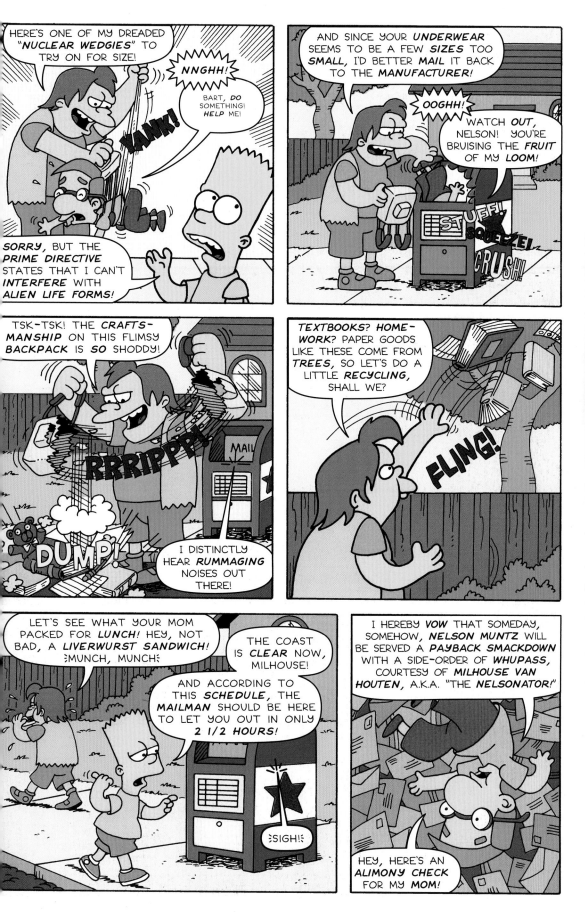